# Caddy-Whack!

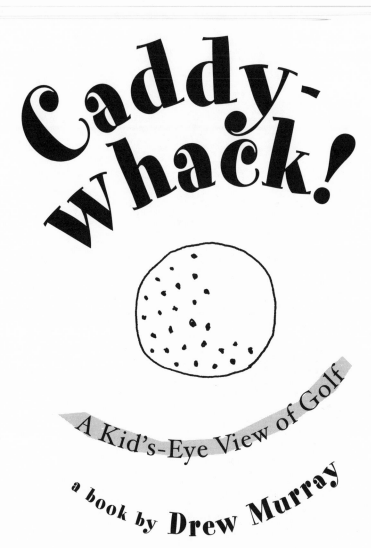

## A Kid's-Eye View of Golf

### a book by Drew Murray

Illustrations by Jeremy Sterling

Clock Tower Press

Clock Tower Press, LLC
320 North Main Street
P.O. Box 310
Chelsea, MI 48118
www.clocktowerpress.com

Printed and bound in the United States.

10 9 8 7 6 5 4 3 2 1


Library of Congress Cataloging-in-Publication Data

Murray, Drew, 1989-
Caddywhack! : a kid's-eye view of golf / by Drew Murray ;
illustrations by Jeremy Sterling.
p. cm.
ISBN 1-932202-00-5
1. Golf. I. Sterling, Jeremy. II. Title.
GV965.M77 2003
796.352–dc21
2002155452

*For Dad, who taught me the game.*

---

# Foreword

---

## By Andy Murray, Drew's Dad

The way I used to think of golf was a couple of six packs in the back of the cart, a couple of buddies, and if I made contact with the ball, I was very happy.

Then one day, a friend of mine and I were sitting in the back yard of our home in Los Angeles with my son Drew. At that time, we lived on the 13th fairway of Rancho Park Golf Course in Los Angeles, which happens to be the busiest golf course in America. Drew was four years old, and he was playing around with a cut-down golf club that my oldest brother had passed down from his kids. He had first seen a driving range at age three when we lived in New York City. He was placing the ball on a tee, and he was just drilling it. His swing was better than mine. This boy who never seemed to have done anything for longer than five minutes other than watch a video, continued to hit that ball for forty-five minutes or an hour. I don't know if he was doing this to make me happy, but it sure did. Because I knew then I had a built-in golf partner for life.

So I took Drew down to the driving range, where we hooked up with the teaching pro. All the old men who were sitting around watching people hit balls would come up and say, "That's the right age to start him at." In a way, I found that I was starting to learn the game again myself, this time looking at it from a whole new point of view— his.

Then one Father's Day morning when Drew was eight, I was awakened to a construction paper card being waved in my face. It was a three-page card, and he had taken my golf magazine and cut out Greg Norman's head and pasted it on my body to illustrate his words. The card talked about golf the way *he* saw it. Every year, he added more to the card, until it grew into a book. Eventually, it became this book.

Along the way, I realized that I had always tried to get Drew to look at golf through *my* eyes, to learn it the way I had been taught, and to do the things you were supposed to do. Instead, he played his own game. He's learned to play golf his way, not my way. And I've learned just get out of the way.

# Table of Contents

# Introduction

**W**hen I was really little, my dad would leave the house every Sunday and go off somewhere with his brothers. They would be gone all day. He always took along this funny equipment— a bunch of metal sticks in a huge bag that was bigger than me. It was too heavy for me to pick up, but there were nice little balls with dimples that I liked to roll along the floor.

Then one day when I was 3, my dad strapped me in my car seat, drove out of New York City, where we lived, and took me along to a place called a driving range. That's when he showed me what the sticks were for. They were called clubs, and the game was called golf. At the driving range, you were supposed to practice hitting golf balls. Dad had brought a little club along for me. It was small, but it was not a toy. It was a real golf club, cut down just for me. Dad showed me how to hold the club by positioning my fingers on the grip. Then he held my hands and helped me swing the club. After a few practice swings, Dad put a ball down. Together, we hit it. At that moment, I would have never realized that golf would become a big part of my life, as well as my dad's. All I knew was that it was fun to swing at something and whack it. Later, I would learn that there is a lot more to golf than just swinging and whacking at the ball. The game of golf requires a lot of thinking, practice, effort, concentration, and talent. You hope.

I think there are a lot of kids like I was, whose dads go off to the golf course, and they wonder what is going on. And there are people who see golf on TV, or watch Tiger Woods and hear about golf, who wish that they could learn more about it. Well, here's the story: I can't tell anybody how to play like Tiger, or hit a 300-yard drive, or get a hole-in-one. But I can tell you what golf is all about, at least as I see it.

So here goes.

FORE!

—Drew Murray

# Chapter 1

# Golf, The Game

You know how in baseball you swing the bat and try to hit the ball as far as you can? Well, golf may seem a lot like that, but it's not. First of all, you usually don't play on a team. Second of all, it's not just about hitting, it's about how you hit.

There is a story about an 800-pound gorilla that hit a golf ball off of the tee to one inch from the hole. But then he hit his next shot just as long as his first shot. Which goes to show you that, in the game of golf, just whacking it as hard as you can is not good enough, believe it or not. The main point of the game is to finish the entire golf course of 18 holes, or sometimes nine, with the lowest possible score you can get— meaning, hitting the ball the least number of times possible. To do this, you have to learn all the shots of golf. There are many different shots: tee shots, fairway shots, chip shots, approach shots, sand shots, and putting.

And that's the least of it.

In golf, even what you wear is important. For instance, you can't usually wear your skateboarding outfit on the golf course, unless it has a shirt with a collar. Some golfers wear shoes with spikes. Imagine football spikes on a dress-up shoe. Spikes are not a rule, they are an option; but there are lots of rules about what you can and can't wear.

There are lots of rules, period. There is an official handbook out there with pages and pages of rules about grass, about water, about sand, sprinklers, stones, even about cleaning the balls. My favorite rule is something called "nearest point of relief." At first, I thought this rule was about finding the closest place to pee on the golf course, but don't even think about it. That one actually has to do with moving the ball away from things that are obstructions on the golf course.

(nearest point of relief)

If you don't like rules, you probably shouldn't play golf. Of course, nobody really likes rules, especially me. That's the funny thing about golf. A lot of people who don't normally like rules follow them on a golf course just for the love of the game. So in one way, the game of golf actually breaks rules because people who don't like rules, as a rule, follow rules on the golf course. Are you following me? Probably not.

Then there's the equipment you need to play the game of golf. The thing to remember here is, golf equipment is either very heavy or very light. The bag that holds the clubs weighs a ton, especially when you have to carry it. It feels like you are carrying Donald Trump's sack of money. The ball itself is light. Unless you get hit in the head with it. Then it feels like Halley's Comet. Once my dad got hit by a golf ball that was hit 200 yards off the course by a really awful golfer. It made a big round bruise the size of a plum on my dad's stomach. We lived at the edge of the golf course and he was lying by the pool of our house at the time, in his bathing suit. Even so, it did not stop him from loving the game.

There are things you need to know about the golf course itself. Unlike a baseball diamond, which has 3 bases, a golf course usually has 18 or 9 very different-shaped areas called holes. They are called holes because, at the end of each one, there is an actual hole in the ground, and that's what you want to get the ball into. The hole itself is very, very small, only about the size of a tennis ball. It is so small, and so far away from where you start, they have to mark it with a flag on a tall pole, otherwise almost nobody would even be able to see it. Getting the ball into one of these holes is what the game is all about. It is very hard to do, and they make it that way on purpose. Holes you can hardly see are just one thing. In fact, they do everything possible to get in the way of the ball reaching the hole. Imagine an obstacle course made out of trees, sand, streams, ponds, hills, brush, whatever. The ball has to make it past all the obstacles to make it to the hole, and what it all adds up to is called a golf course. But the harder it is, the better golfers like it. Go figure.

The most important thing you need to know about the game of golf is, it's not just a game. When you play golf, nature takes over your body, and all the good things in life become you, and you have not a care in the world— except for the conflict between you and the hole. You think about all the ups of your life, and forget all the downs, and you say to yourself, "I have a great life."

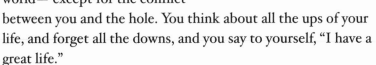

On the golf course, you think about all the things that you don't ever normally think about, like "Why is the grass green?" And "Why are Warheads so sour?" One time when I was on the golf course, I was having a great round. No matter what happened, I just kept going, like the Energizer Bunny. All my problems went away. It just freed my mind. In school, I hadn't been able to figure out some math problems. It was like there was this mental block between me and an A. But my mind was freed for just that time, and, all of a sudden, everything just came to me. And that made me feel like, if I could do this on the golf course, I could surely do it in school, too. Golf is like that.

When you play with your friends, it's not a competition with you and another person, it's more a competition of you and yourself. Golf is a great game, because, on the golf course, unlike the rest of the world, the only person who can put you down is yourself.

# Chapter 2

# It's In The Bag

The golf bag looks mysterious from the outside, like a giant cylinder with legs and a strap. Someone from outer space might think it was an ally. The golf bag is used to carry your golfing equipment across the entire golf course.

Many things are carried in the bag. The most important thing it carries are the golf clubs. Other equipment is also carried in a golf bag. The contents consist of, not in any special order:

**1. Golf tees.**

These are small objects that are used to hold up a golf ball when you tee off. That's why they're called tees.

tee-rex

mr. tee

tee ball

tee shirt

cup o' tee

## 2. Divot fixers.

When you create a divot, which is
when you hit a golf ball and it lands
very hard on the ground, it will make a
dent that looks like a small crater. If you are
having a bad golf day, you can do the same thing
with your club. You use the divot fixer to cover up the dent
with other grass, to keep the green flat. Divot fixers look
like small forks, but do not use them to eat with, due
to the risk of fertilizer
poisoning.

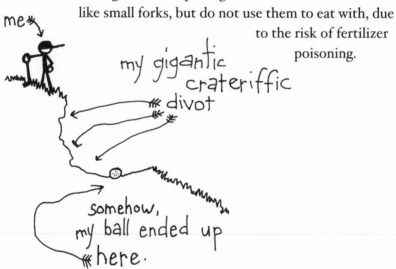

## 3. Ball markers.

You don't actually mark your ball with these, so don't try
it. Besides, they don't write. Ball markers look like mini-Frisbees
with a spike at the bottom. They are used to mark where your
ball was on the green when your ball is in the way of the other
person's putt.

**4. Golf balls.**

Why do they have dimples all over them? Beats me.

**5. Clubs.**

You can belong to a golf club-- or you can hit with one. The hitting kind are what you hit the ball with. You can hit other things with a golf club, like car windows or piano keys, but I don't recommend it. It could ruin your golf swing.

The rule is that you can only have 14 clubs in your bag. If you want more than 14 clubs, tough cookies for you. They won't allow it. If you bring more than 14 clubs on the course, the Club Police will ride up in a golf cart and remove the extras from your bag. So try it at your own risk.

**There are three main different kinds of clubs:**

**Woods.**

Believe it or not, these clubs are not always made out of wood. They are called woods because they used to be made out of wood. I would think. These have big, fat heads and are used for hitting off the tee or for long holes. Always ask yourself: "How much wood could Tiger Woods chuck if Tiger Woods could chuck wood?"

**Irons.**

These are usually used to hit the ball on the fairway or the rough. This club looks like a blade on a stick.

They do not hit the ball as long as woods. There are many kinds of irons, and all of them are in the bag at once. The lower the number, the farther they can be used to hit. It helps to know your numbers.

One time, I mistook my 4-iron for a 9-iron. I hit the ball 40 yards past the green. Do not underestimate the power of irons. They play a big part in this game, just like the big peach in *James and the Giant Peach*.

### Putters.

A putter is somewhat of a mallet that is used once you are on the green to gently tap the ball into the hole. That is one of the problems with this club—you have to get to the green to use it. And then, once you are there, a lot of things can happen when the ball is on the way to the hole. For instance, your ball can hit a barn.

Or, you could misread the green. The green could have said, "Hit the ball this way," and you hit it that-a-way.

### 6. Club covers.

These are like socks for golf clubs. They are used to protect the metal or wood of the club. Sometimes club covers can have college emblems or animal faces. Tiger Woods has one that looks like a tiger. Some have little fuzzy balls on top, like a ski hat. There is no such thing as a way cool club cover.

### 7. Towel.

The towel is critical. It is used to clean golf balls and clubs. And your hands. In golf, cleaning the ball or clubs can be more important than even you being clean yourself, because cleaning the ball or club affects how much spin and accuracy you have on your shots.

### 8. Gloves.

They are used to protect your hands from getting blisters from the grip. You are not O.J. Simpson. Use gloves wisely.

### 9. Umbrella.

If it starts raining, you keep playing until there's lightning. If you are out there and lightning strikes, don't hold the umbrella up in the air. You're not going to get better TV reception.

### 10. Hat.

There are two main styles of hats for golf: baseball and visor. The only other style is the type that Jesper Parnevik wears, which is a baseball cap with a brim that is out of control.

Everyone wears a hat on the golf course. I have no clue why. Maybe one day long ago, some fellow walked in out of nowhere and said, "Everyone, let's wear hats!"

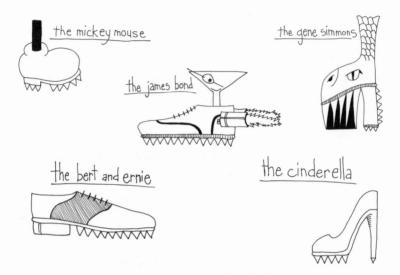

the mickey mouse

the gene simmons

the james bond

the bert and ernie

the cinderella

### 11. Golf shoes.

These are fancy-looking shoes with spikes on the bottom. Do not use them to kick your older brother.

### 12. Optionals:

- water bottle
- windbreaker. In case you break wind.
- food. Be careful not to put an egg salad sandwich in your golf bag. Things could get ugly if it falls to the bottom.
- first aid. Band-Aids, ACE bandage, ice pack, aspirin. If you get too far in the rough, vaccines.

## 13. No-no's:

- cell phone or beeper. Noise is bad on the course. Golfers lose concentration and they could break a club.
- radios. Golfers do not like to hear annoying songs. They think any song is annoying.
- toys. Superheroes don't play golf.
- computers. Slow downloads cause backups on the golf course.
- TV. The only thing you want to watch is the ball.
- homework. Too stressful. 2 + 2 = bogey.

A professional golfer's golf bag has enough in it to last him an entire round of golf, no matter what happens. The contents of a pro's golf bag would last a normal person the length of a camping trip. The professional has to be prepared for rain, sleet, snow, floods, or anything. One time, the famous caddy Fluff Cowan let me look into a bag he was carrying in a PGA tournament for a golf star. It was like an airplane cargo hold. When I looked deep inside, a little man named Jim-Bob was living off what was in the bag.

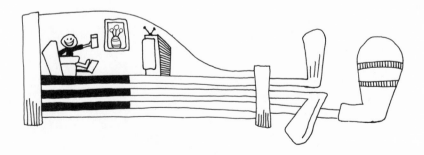

# Chapter 3

# Golf Manners

**M**ind your manners! Consideration for other players is a very important part of golf. In fact, how you act on a golf course is almost as important as how well you play. You could be a great golfer, but if you have awful manners, no one will like you and you will have to play by yourself, which is like never being picked for the team. You can be an awful golfer with good manners, and everyone will like you and want to play with you. That's just the way it is in golf.

Golf manners are not like dinner manners. Here's what they are like:

**No yelling.** Yelling gets you into trouble because it distracts other golfers. For instance, if someone was in the middle of their backswing when, all of a sudden, you yelled out, "Juicy Fruit, the taste the taste the taste is gonna move you!" the person who was hitting the ball could accidentally — because of you — hit it into a sand trap. When you watch golf matches on TV, you may notice that the announcers all whisper. This is why.

**Learn the golf clap.** Normal clapping is loud and makes a slapping noise. Golf clapping is gently tapping your hands together as if you had an already-blown piece of bubble gum between them, and you were trying to clap without popping it. This takes some practice.

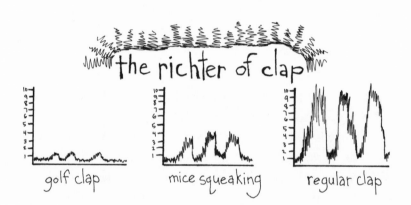

the richter of clap

golf clap          mice squeaking          regular clap

**Do not step in the line of someone else's ball.** First of all, only a very dumb person would stand in the line of someone else's drive. You might get a boo-boo. If someone else is putting, and you were to step in the line of their putt, you could accidentally change the direction of the ball's roll. This would mean that they could miss their putt. Result: steam will come out of their ears and they will charge like a bull.

**Farthest goes first.** When you are hitting the ball to the hole, the person whose ball is farthest away gets to take the first turn. This is like the consolation prize for hitting the shortest shot.

**First dibs.** The person who has the lowest score on the last hole that you have played gets to play first on the next hole. "Rock, scissors, paper, shoot!" does not apply on the golf course.

No cutting in. Even if you are in a hurry, you should not barge through the group of people ahead of you. You can ask if you can play through, and maybe they will let you— but maybe they won't— like Mother May I. If they say no, you have to stay where you are. On the other hand, if you are play-ing, you can be a good guy, be patient and let the other players go ahead of you. Your reward will be that you get to stand by and crack jokes about how bad they are playing.

**No drag racing the cart.** Actually, I've done this before. I was in a cart with my grandfather, racing my dad, on a short par 3.

We were going downhill, so I decided to drive really, really fast. I was only 6, so I didn't have very good control. I accidentally ran over a ball washer. You should not do this because you could earn yourself a free trip in the ambulance.

**Never throw a club.** This is the A-1 rule. Also, never play with people who do throw clubs. They're usually jerks. Also, you can be hit by a flying Callaway.

**Rake your sandtrap.** Always rake your sandtrap before you leave. How would you like it if your ball landed in someone else's divot because they were too lazy to rake the sandtrap?

**No spikes in the clubhouse.** Golf shoes should be left in your bag or your locker. That way, they cannot escape and invade the clubhouse.

**Always wear a collared shirt.** You should always wear a collared shirt on the golf course, no matter what the circumstances. Everybody who plays golf wears a collared shirt. It is the unofficial uniform of golf (along with the hat). This is something that has been passed on from generation to generation, probably invented by the cavemen when they learned to weave cloth.

**No distracting.** Especially when someone else is swinging or putting. No jingling coins. No swearing. No singing. No dancing. No crying. No slurping a drink.

**If ya gotta go.** Be sure to pee under a tree that's got some coverage.

# Chapter 4

# The Rules

I n golf, the rules are followed by all golfers. It's cool to follow the rules. If you really want to get into the details, there is an official book put out by the United States Golf Association that has over 100 pages of rules. I have actually read this book, or at least some of it. So let me save you the trouble and give you a few of the highlights.

### Address the ball.

Addressing a golf ball is not like addressing a letter. You don't write "100 Fairway Drive" on it before you hit it. When you address the ball, you put your feet in position and ground the club. That's all there is to it.

### Play it where it lies.

If you hit a ball and it lands in a certain spot, you have to play it from that spot. For instance, if your ball lands in a tree, you either have to climb the tree and hit it out, or take a penalty and go to jail. The other player advances to Boardwalk.

## No mowing.

You are not allowed to change the grass around the ball. This means no picking grass, pushing it down, mowing it, weed-whacking it, or bulldozing it.

## No subtraction.

The numbers on your scorecard must add up at the end of the game. Every player has to keep his or her own scorecard. You cannot bring your accountant along to do it for you, unless, of course your accountant is playing in your group.

## Pool rules.

If you hit the ball into a water hazard or pool, the ball must be treading water— meaning, part of it must be above the water— for you to be able to try to play it. Otherwise, you have to take penalty strokes and do a lap in the pool.

## Tee time.

You can only use a tee when you are in the tee box—that is where you hit your drives from. The rest of the time, you have to hit it off the grass. You absolutely can't use a tee while you are putting. Don't try flying it into the hole; it won't work. Usually.

**Marking your ball.**

Players should make sure they can tell which ball is theirs. It is very bad to hit someone else's ball; do so at your own risk because you will get penalty strokes. You can use different colors or symbols on your ball. Most people just use a dot, but there is nothing in the rules that say you can't use a hangman, a skull and crossbones, Flameboy or Wet Willy. Think of it as a tattoo for the ball— golf balls are rough and tough.

**Animals on the course.**

Many animals have golf courses as their natural habitat. You may see gophers, woodchucks, squirrels, beavers, or, if you are very far out-of-bounds, rhinoceros. If you hit your ball into a gopher hole, sorry— it doesn't count as a hole-in-one. You do get a few breaks. If your ball falls into a hole that is dug by a French Poodle, that is considered abnormal, and you can replace it.

However, you rarely see French Poodles on golf courses.

### Obtaining relief.

This has to do with things that are in your way that block the ball. If the ball is not in or on the thing that is in the way, the thing can be moved. If the ball is in or on it, the ball can be picked up, and the thing can be moved. Then you are allowed to drop the ball or put it as near as possible to where it was, as long as you do not put the ball any closer to the hole. Let's say your ball lands on a lawn flamingo. First of all, this is trouble because if this happens, you are not on the green, you are on somebody's lawn. Aside from that, you are allowed to move the flamingo, drop the ball where the flamingo was, and hit from there. Good luck.

### Unplayable ball.

If your ball ends up in the middle of somebody's Caesar salad, then don't worry about it: you're already on the green. Otherwise, you can drop the ball two club lengths from where the ball was.

### Lost ball.

Sometimes you might lose your ball. The worst place to lose it is in a Porta-Potti. If that happens, forget it even if you have to take a penalty stroke.

**Dropping the ball.**

In football, baseball, or basketball, it is never good to drop the ball. That is where the phrase, "dropping the ball" came from, meaning, "you screwed up." Same in golf. When you have to drop the ball in golf, it means you screwed up. A situation that would call for a ball drop might be that your ball lands in water, or on a stag moose. In these kinds of cases, you get to stand up straight, hold out one arm at shoulder height, and drop the ball from your hand. Then you can play it where it lies, hoping not to screw up yet again.

**No cheating.**

This means no kicking the ball closer to the hole, no hitting the ball without counting strokes, no hitting the ball while it is still moving, no carrying it out of the rough in your pocket and dropping it off on the fairway, no erasing your score and writing in a better one.

**No illegal equipment.**

You might think you could hit the ball farther with a baseball bat, but forget it. The rules say you have to use certain types of clubs and balls. Anything else is banned. There is one club that was banned because the face of it was so big and so

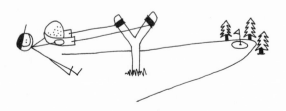

thin it was like a trampoline. And you can't put a candle in a golf hole and use a heat-seeking ball. The golf authorities are a lot more specific. You can torture yourself to death with the details. For example, here is an exact quote about the rules of club alignment from the USGA Rules of Golf book:

"Except for putters, all of the heel portion of the club shall lie within 0.625 inches (15.88mm) of the plane containing the axis of the straight part of the shaft and the intended (horizontal) line of play." English, please!!

**Breaking the rules.**

There is even a rule for this: Breaking a rule will cost you. Depending on the rule and how you break it, it could cost you strokes, or even the entire hole. It's the exact opposite of what happens when you don't follow the rules on a test in school. There, they take off points. In golf, they add strokes.

# Chapter 5

# A Golf Course Is Not Just For Golf

One of the great things about golf is all the things you can do on a golf course while you are playing the game. First of all, although you can play golf anytime at all by yourself, you can also use your tee time as a time to get together with your friends or family. A game of golf is one of the best times to talk. A golf course is very big, making it difficult to listen in on other people, and it is impossible to bug, so you can talk about things you don't want other people to hear under any circumstances, like the fact that you have rubber sheets, or you flunked woodshop. Watching how people act on the golf course tells you a lot about them. While you are reading the greens, you can also read the person you are playing with. For instance, if he lies on his scorecard, he might just take the Oreos off your lunch tray when you're not looking. If someone misses the ball or has a bad shot and wants to take it over, he might also say that the dog ate his homework so he deserves an extra day. If someone throws a

tied up wimp
throwing competition

club because he's not playing well, he
might throw the board if you beat
him at Monopoly. Or he might throw
you, if you are smaller than him. On the
other hand, if someone offers to carry your bag
for 18 holes, you can be pretty sure that this is the
kind of person who would offer you their lunch
money, if you lost yours.

You also learn things about yourself on the
golf course. When you have to make a long putt, and
you sink it, you learn that you can do well under pressure. You
learn about making decisions. If you are 125 yards out, with
the wind in your face, and you usually hit a 7-iron from there,
you have to use your judgment on what club to use— if you
should bring it one club lower, or two clubs lower. You have to
figure out how hard the wind is blowing to make that deci-
sion, just like when you have to figure out how hard a test is
going to be in order to judge how much you should study for
it. When you try to get out of a sand trap and you're using
your sand wedge, and you can't get out with it
because it's falling short, you might try blasting
it out with your driver— or you might try to
throw it out and take the penalty, because
you're so frustrated. Or you could use your
head, and give the sand wedge a few
more tries, maybe hit with a slight
inside-to-out stroke, hitting one inch
behind the ball. To me, that's like what
happens in life, when suddenly you can't

HELP

english                    math
                           history

manage all the homework that's been piling up on top of you. Instead of trying to muscle your way out by blowing it off, pretending you don't have to worry about anything, when you're actually just digging that hole deeper, you could look at it a different way; instead of just plowing straight through your homework, you could try to do it from a different angle, like doing one assignment at a time, and working your way out of it. Or like in baseball, when you try to throw the ball before you really catch it in your glove, you'll miss the play.

You learn to be honest with yourself on the golf course. For instance, if you have a ball that is up against a tree, you kick it out into the fairway, because you think you can get away with it because nobody is looking, you will never learn how to play your way out of it. It's like in school, when you cheat on a test, you don't really learn the information, and you might never know it. Not to mention the guilt that happens when you cheat,

which is like a tarantula eating you from the inside out, starting with your heart.

When you are playing golf, making the right shot can make you think about the rights and wrongs in the rest of your life. When you try to fly the ball and stop it two inches from the cup, instead of running it on the green and stopping it two feet away, and you end up flying the ball completely over the green, it reminds you of what happens when you make one choice and not another. Maybe you think, "I should have tried the other shot." That leads you to thinking about other things you might have done that might be wrong, that maybe you should have done differently— like picking a person to be on your team because you thought he was a better athlete, instead of someone else. Later you think back on what you did and why— "Maybe I should have let that other guy play on my team. Maybe he felt left out or not wanted." You learn things about making choices.

When you hit your ball into the rough and have to make it back to the fairway or the green, you learn what it takes to make it through obstacles. There might be a tree in your way that you have to get around. There might be a big bush blocking your way. But you figure out how to do it. That gets you to thinking: you wish you could buy an Alex Rodriguez jersey baseball card. But you don't have enough money. How are you going to get the card? You figure out a way to work your way to buying it. Maybe you get some odd jobs, or do some babysitting to earn the cash. Eventually, you figure out a way to get the card, just like you figured out a way to get out of the rough.

A golf course has many of
the elements of the universe
itself. If you were really strand-
ed on a golf course because
you were with a record slow
foursome and it took you
three weeks to play 36 holes,
you could probably survive by for-
aging. If there was a maple tree, you could get syrup. There
may be fish in the water hazard. There are plenty of twigs and
leaves to start a fire. And if things get really bad, there's always
the halfway house. The halfway house is a place located
between the front nine and the back nine where you can stop
for food and drink. It is not cool to pack a lunch on the golf
course. You will never see Jack Nicklaus walking a fairway
with a bologna sandwich in his hand. He would much rather
forage in the rough than be seen doing this. Take your cue
from the Golden Bear.

The clubhouse actually is a place that can take care of
almost anything you need. It is like a mini-mall with a very, very
expensive restaurant. Like school, the clubhouse has lockers
where you can keep your things. But, unlike school, you have
to be a member of the club to use the lockers. There is usually
a bar at the clubhouse, and a porch where you can sit with
your drink and talk about your ten-stroke holes and your five-
putts, and how you missed the green from five yards out, or
got a hole-in-one, but on the wrong hole.

Being on the golf course is also a great way to get exercise
without going to the gym and pumping iron. What would you

| working out | golfing |
|---|---|
| sweat | swing |
| free weights | cheap snacks |
| stinky gym | great outdoors |
| sore muscles | suntan |
| stationary exercise bike | golf cart, the ultimate vehicle |
| "no pain, no gain." | "no pan, no cheese sandwich at the halfway house." |
| healthy balanced diet | yeah, right!!! |

rather do— sweat or swing? The game of golf exercises almost every muscle in a person's body. Walking the fairways works out your legs. Swinging the club exercises your upper body. Putting exercises your arms. Waiting for the old guys in the foursome in front of you exercises your patience.

The golf cart is possibly the most versatile vehicle on the planet. It can be used as a tent, a bachelor pad, a fishing boat, a bus, or even an airplane. Golf carts can handle almost any kind of terrain, from flat grass to paved roads, hills, or a McDonald's drive-through. The only kind of terrain that is not advisable is the green. No one wants to hit out of a tire track. The great thing about driving a golf cart is that whenever you are at the wheel of one, you feel like one of those beautiful people in a Jet Ski commercial, laughing, with your hair blowing in the wind. It doesn't even matter what your score is.

Finally, you can get a great tan on a golf course. All you have to do is carry suntan lotion with a zero SPF and pretend that the sand trap is a beach. The longer you spend in the trap, the darker your tan. Most golfers have great tans. Turn on any golf show and see for yourself.

Still, in spite of all the things you can do on the golf course besides play golf, the game itself is the best part. Golf is a kind of magic circle. The greenskeepers take care of the grass; which the balls land on, and we hit off of; the clubs hit the ball; and we swing the clubs that hit the ball. We learn how to play the game from our elders, who have learned the game from their elders. Golf is a game you can never stop working on. There's always something to change or improve. Golf is really a game with no beginning and no end. It's a circle. The Circle of Golf.

# Chapter 6

# The Golf Community

**M**any different kinds of people can be found on a golf course. It is like a community. Everyone is there for a reason, and does a particular job. It's good to know who these people are. Every one of them can help your game in some way.

The golf pro is the one who passes on his knowledge to help you learn the game of golf. He is the all-wise, all-powerful, and all-mighty. He can show you how to hold your grip, or the correct angle to swing your club, or how to get height on your drive or spin on your ball. These are all secrets, and they will share them with you, if you listen. They give you hope and make you feel good about yourself. A playing lesson with a golf pro is like a four-hour pep talk. The golf pros are the ones who make the professionals professionals. They are like your teachers, but they will never give you detention, even if you mistake your 5-iron for a sand wedge. I once had a lesson from one of the best golf pros, Kip Putterbaugh. It was like a message from God.

All professional golfers have caddies. A caddy carries your clubs and cleans them off, helps you read the green, figure out how far your shot has to go, pick a club, or determine how strong the wind is blowing. Caddies are very wise. They have seen many things. They are sort of like the elders in Japan— respected for their experience and knowledge. Caddies have seen every shot that exists. They have seen duck hooks, regular hooks, slices, tops, skulls, pulls, pop-ups, even whiffs. They have stood by their player in rain,

duck hook

snow, sleet, hail, sun, darkness, wind, freezing cold, blistering heat, even lightning. They have seen smiles, tears, high-fives, and money changing hands. They know good jokes. Caddies probably know more about the game of golf than most professionals.

fore!!!

After many good rounds with a caddy, eternal bonding may be achieved. After all, this is the person who helped you get a low score.

The greenskeeper tends to the golf course, makes sure it's in shape, and is responsible for the placement of the cup. Who knows what evil lies

within the mind of a greenskeeper. The guy in the pro shop is there to sell you the golf merchandise you need to play the game. He can sell you anything from clubs to tees to visors. But he does not have the final word. Before buying clubs, consult with your golf pro. Before buying a hat, look in the mirror.

The chef in the halfway house is a key team member. He is responsible for keeping you alive while you play golf. All halfway house chefs are gourmet caliber. For example, halfway through a golf game, absolutely nothing in the world tastes better than their hot dogs, Snapples, or extra-greasy cheeseburgers.

The unknown hero. This is the guy on the driving range who drives into the line of fire to pick up all the golf balls that have fallen in the line of duty. He risks his life in a metal cage on wheels just so you can practice your swing.

There are as many different types of players as flavors at Baskin-Robbins, and that's a lot. First of all, there are the scratch golfers. These are the supergolfers with handicaps below zero. They break 80 almost every time they play, and have been known to shoot in the 60s. They like to play with other people who are at their caliber. Not usually you.

Watch out for bad golfers. Actually, you don't need to see them. You can hear them. These are the people who yell out "Fore!" at least twice each hole.

Some golfers are practical jokers. They like to cough loudly when other people hit, hide people's balls, or hit exploding golf balls when they tee off. The reason they do this is so no one will notice how badly they are playing.

Then there are extreme golfers. These are the people who play golf whenever possible, under any circumstances. You will find them on the golf course at night, using glow-in-the-dark balls and flagsticks, stripes marking the fairways, and glow strips on their carts. Extreme golfers also play in the snow, using colored balls; in the rain, wearing wetsuits; and in the desert, practicing their sand trap shots. Nothing keeps the extreme golfer from the course. He is like a giant bowling ball rolling down a greased lane.

Another type of golfer is the getaway golfer. These golfers use the golf course to get away from things like helping their wives with spring cleaning, or raking the leaves in the yard, or almost anything they don't want to do. They can be found on the golf course in the earliest morning, at dawn when the golf course opens. Here is what they think: "I can get in a round of golf before anybody wakes up, then I can go home, get back into bed, and sleep through emptying out the garage." I know this works because my dad did it once.

Finally, there is the golfer I call Golf Man. Golf Man lives for golf. Every time you go to the golf course, Golf Man is there. He eats, sleeps, drinks, works, plays, and thinks golf. He wears collared shirts with golf course logos on them everywhere, not just on the golf course. He can quote golf scores of all the greats, and he knows every kind of golf trivia, like how many times Bobby Jones won the U.S. Open, or how many pink shirts Arnold Palmer has in his closet. Golf Man needs to get a life.

In other words, the golf course is kind of like Disney World. Disney World has every kind of person imaginable, and even some you can't imagine until you get there. When all these different types of people get together in one place, you learn how to act in different situations, how to react to things that other people do, how to accept people for what they are, and not what they aren't. When you are on a golf course, it doesn't matter where people are from or what they do for a living.

Golf helps you learn how other people make you what you are. For instance, the greenskeeper may not seem important at first. You may not even notice him. But without the greenskeeper, there would be no hole. and you couldn't sink clutch putts from 60 feet out. You couldn't hit 300-yard drives if there was no fairway. And you couldn't nail incredible chip shots out of the sand trap if there was no sand. The greenskeeper puts those things in order. It's the small things in life that make the world big.

# Chapter 7

# Hitting The Ball

If you can't hit the ball, you can't play golf. The game of golf is mostly about hitting the golf ball where you want it to go, and getting it to go into the hole. It looks like it should be easy to hit a golf ball, because it looks so innocent and small that you think it can't possibly do anything to you. But it can make you frustrated, angry, sad, happy, even powerful. It can make you feel like a king— or like the jester that performs for the king, the guy everybody laughs at because he looks moronic.

Hitting a golf ball is not as easy as it looks, take it from me. There are more than a million things that can go wrong— actually, there are an infinite number of things that can go wrong between your backswing and making contact with the ball. You could swing too inside out and cause yourself to hit a hook. Or too outside in and hit a slice. Or a competitor could stand behind you with a horn in his hand, blowing it during your backswing, and cause you to jump on top of the ball. If you are professional, the gallery could all jingle their keys in their pocket and make you very nervous,

movie: my baby boy's great round of golf

| scene: bogey on the 9th | take: 29 |

causing you to chilly-dip a shot. Or your mom could pull up on a cart with a video camera and cause you to be filled with so much embarrassment that you whiff it. That's a golf term for missing the ball completely. This happened to me once on vacation. My mom followed me on the front nine and I shot a 52. After she left, I shot a 42 on the back nine. Moral: if you want to hit the ball, leave your mom at home— especially if she's packing a video cam.

### The Fundamentals of Hitting

#### 1. Your grip.

A grip is how you hold the club. When you look at a person holding a golf club, it's like their fingers are tied up in a monkey fist knot around it. The reason their fingers are knotted is for safety, so that the club will not go flying out of their hands and hit the snack cart lady. The correct way to hold the club is by using what is called an interlock grip. This is when you grip the club and interlock your pinkie and index finger into a monkey fist knot. But when you are just starting to play

the game, it is OK to hold the club however you want. An example of this is the baseball grip, like the way you hold a bat, which is the way I started. However, if you actually tried to play golf with a baseball bat, they might have to change the rules to allow people to stand on the golf course holding giant signs saying, "HIT IT HERE."

### 2. Your feet.

Feet are the engine of the golf game. You may think feet are just for walking, but they can be used for other things, like getting foot massages, kicking a soccer ball, and lining up correctly on the golf course. When you line up your shot, you want to have your feet about shoulder-width apart, set together like train tracks, aimed toward your target, parallel to your club face. This is a very important aspect of the game. At least that's what they tell you. If you do not do that, your ball could end up at the halfway house in someone's sandwich.

Comfy feet are the key to golf. If your feet hurt, then you will change their position to make them feel better, causing you to hit the ball in the wrong place and, in the end, causing you to feel worse. To keep your feet comfy, you need the following: shoes and socks.

Golf shoes look dorky. But they are actually engineered by NASA. If you are walking on the moon and you fall into a crater, you have to be able to land with comfort. The same is true on the golf course, when you fall into a sand trap.

The golf shoe is Batman, and the sock is like Robin. Batman could never have beaten Joker without the help of Robin. And the golf shoe cannot help you beat your opponent without its sock— unless you are losing and you take your shoe off and beat him over the head with it. Hey, it can happen!

### 3. Taking aim.

Taking aim is short and sweet. Aim where you want the ball to go.

### 4. The practice swing.

Many of us have heard from our basketball or baseball coaches that practice makes perfect. But the way that I think of it is, perfect practice makes perfect. You may have noticed while watching golfers play that before they hit each shot, they take a practice swing. Maybe you think they were missing the ball. But what they are actually doing is visualizing their next shot, the way a Buddha visualizes a frog on a lily pad. In the golfer's mind, the ball is carried by a stork like a baby, and dropped gently into the hole, giving birth to a hole-in-one.

### 5. The real swing.

This is the swing that counts. Once you address the ball, each swing you take is a stroke on your scorecard. So don't miss! Of course, you keep your own scorecard, so there is always a chance that you might not record each stroke you take. This is a bad move, because if you do that, your golf clubs will grow longer with each unrecorded stroke, just like Pinocchio's nose. There are some people out there playing golf that should be driving 18-wheelers to carry their clubs, instead of carts.

## 6. Follow-through.

The follow-through is what you do with your swing after making contact with the ball. Almost every sport that uses a ball requires a follow-through, even croquet. Follow-through is key to making your swing look good. You want to end up with your club over your shoulder, your body aiming down the fairway, your back toe on its tippy-toe, the sun at 35 degrees northwest, with a black cat falling out of a tree. If you don't do this, everyone will say, "Eeew, he has a nasty swing."

# Chapter 8

# Getting Around The Course

Unlike most sports, in which there is usually only one way to get around, there are many ways to get around a golf course. When you watch a game of golf, you may see people walking around the course, climbing out of a sand trap, driving

a golf cart, or even swimming out of a lake— or if you look closely enough, you may see little kids pulling their fathers around the course. The reason there are so many ways of getting around the golf course is because there are so many surfaces and situations that you have to cover. You never know what you may encounter, so you have to be ready for everything, even clawing yourself out of a pot bunker in Scotland.

### 1. Walking.

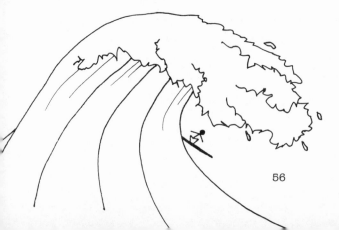

This is my least favorite way of getting around the golf course. This takes effort. The average golf course can be as much as 7,200 yards long over 18 holes. That's a lot of steps. Instead of placing your bag on the back of your golf cart and speeding around the course, you may be lugging your golf bag on your back. This is where the expression "the whole nine yards" came from, except in this case, it is the whole 7,200 yards.

### 2. Climbing.

There are two ways of climbing on a golf course: out of a sand trap and into a tree. Neither one is good.

### 3. Swimming.

Just in case it's a hot summer day, pack your swim trunks along with your golf gear and take a cool, refreshing dip at the gunk-filled, alligator-infested lake at your local course. Surf's up! Hopefully, you're a good enough golfer to skip the scuba gear.

### 4. Driving.

One of the first things you see when you walk onto a golf course is all the golf carts lined up, ready for the taking. But you have to be 14 years old to drive a golf cart. If you play by the rules. Right now, for the sake of this book, I am theoretically 14, so I can speak on the subject. You steer it with a wheel. Maybe you had a toy remote control car. This is nothing like it. A golf cart is bigger, faster, and a lot more fun. A golf cart is used to carry your golf bags, your drinks, your balls and accessories, and it has a basket for your headcovers.

Three people, tops, can fit in a cart, unless your friend is very flexible and willing to be shoved into your bag.

## THE DREAM MACHINE

The Dream Machine would be equipped with two flat-screen TVs; a PS2 with all the games; a minisub Z filled with Dr. Pepper, Gatorade, and Cherry Coke; a sno-cone machine; a juicer; a grill; a computer; a boom box; a DVD player; an MP3 player; a digital camera to record your swing; and the complete

contents of a candy vending machine. The cart would go at least 40 miles per hour. As far as I know, they do not make this yet. What are they waiting for?

# Chapter 9

# Hazards Of Golf

**H**ave you ever seen the movie *Indiana Jones*? In the movie, the main character has to weave his way through every kind of trap you can imagine, such as quicksand, snakes, landslides, alligators, flames, and booby traps. When you're playing on the golf course, it's as though you are Indiana Jones. The idea is to hit the ball to avoid the hazards of the course and get the ball to a safe spot, to prepare yourself for your next attack. Easier said than done!

There may not be flames or boiling oil on a golf course, but the hazards you will find are almost as scary. Don't think a seagull can't be dangerous. They can swoop in and take your ball and it could cost you a $2.50 replacement ball.

And you feel just like Indiana Jones when you bravely crawl up the side of a sand trap on your belly.

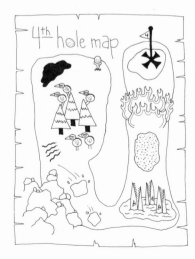

There are many types of hazards in the game of golf. The most common hazard is probably the sand trap. A sand trap is like a giant sand box, except you can play in it at any age, and it isn't actually fun. Sand traps are normally positioned on the fairway area of the rough, and their job is to stop you at any cost. A sand trap is like a giant magnet for a golf ball. The ball could be flying straight to the fairway and all of a sudden, through no fault of your own, it veers off course and—

plunk!— falls into the sand trap. Once it's in the sand, you can't use a bucket or a shovel to get it out. That would be too easy. No, you have to climb in there and make your way to the ball like Lawrence of Arabia crossing the Sahara. Once you get to the ball, you have to play it as it lies, meaning you cannot move the ball out of the trap in order to give yourself a better lie. To do that is cheating and will cost you strokes. When people are playing alone, they normally do that anyhow.

Water is another hazard. They say that water covers more than a third of the earth's surface, and you can believe it on a golf course. You have ponds, streams, even oceans to get between you and your target, the hole. Your job is to hit the ball nice and high over the water. The problem is, alligators might jump out of the water and snag your ball. Or the ball

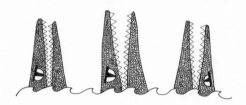

could drop into the water and sink straight to the bottom, never to be seen again. The golfer cannot carry scuba gear, flippers, life vests, or goggles as part of his or her equipment. Even if you do, it would be almost impossible to find your ball amidst all the flagsticks, rusty clubs thrown in anger, and millions of other golf balls that have become part of the underwater ecology of the water hazard. Another kind of water is what is called casual water. Casual water is not a water hazard that dresses down on Friday. It is a water you can see on the ground that interferes with your stance. Because of this, you can get an optional free drop. This means you can drop the ball in an area where there is no water surrounding your feet, and you do not have to pay $1.99.

Trees are the tallest hazards you will find on the golf course, unless you are playing miniature golf and find yourself under a giant windmill. Any kind of tree can be a hazard. They include ancient redwoods, weeping willows, giant elms, proud oaks, Christmas trees, palm trees, and even harmless-looking bushes. The tree walks around the golf course when you're not looking, placing itself directly in front of your shot.

The ball has the following reaction: it hits  the tree trunk and bounces off, never to be seen again. Meanwhile, your game is being taken away from you by a large piece of brainless wood.

Sprinkler heads sound harmless, but get you and your ball wet, causing you to destroy the sprinkler head in a fury, thus destroying your game.

Stones are considered hazards if they come in contact with the ball. Your club could act like a slingshot, hitting your partner in the head with the stone. For this reason, the rules allow you to move the stone. Unless it is a two-ton boulder. Then you need a couple of sticks of dynamite and a box of matches and you'll be fine, provided you make it back to the clubhouse before the fuse blows.

Animals can be mischievously hazardous on the golf course. Do not trust anything that looks like a rat with a bushy tail. Salamanders also like to burrow into the ground. Beware if there is a salamander lying on your golf ball. It might decide to burrow down, through the grass and dirt, deep into the molten lava core at the center of the earth, taking your ball with it.

Homo sapiens are possibly the most annoying hazards. In the middle of your backswing, a person on another hole who has made a long putt may start yelling and screaming with joy, causing you to jump and slice your shot. You never know what a person will do, which makes people a dangerous hazard. For instance, if your partner steps on your ball, that is sure to lower its self-esteem, resulting in its total refusal to cooperate. Golf hazards teach you a lot. They teach you to never give up and always keep trying. Whatever you do, there will always be things in your way that you have to get around, and you will always have to know how to get in, get out, or go around them. For example, on the playground during recess, there is always a bully who picks on you. You have some choices— you can fight him, talk to him, or go to school in a chicken suit so nobody knows who you are. But at some point, you are going to have to face that bully and stand up to him. In the same way, you are going to have to confront that sand trap. You have to be ready, when that time comes, to get yourself out and on the green.

In golf, you take chances and try to go around a hazard, but you won't always make it. Somehow, you always end up in a hazard at some point. You've just gotta deal with it!

# Chapter 10

# The World Of Golf

The golf club is a small world in itself. It consists of everything you need to keep yourself busy for as long as you need. Some people have wandered off into the deep, deep rough of the golf course and never been seen again. Others have gone into pro shops and emerged 10 years later unrecognizable, their body covered with tags. A golf course is in many ways just like a mini-amusement park: the golf carts are the roller coasters; the fairway is like the boardwalk; the pro shop is like a candy shop to a golfer. Let's go on a little tour to see what this small world is really like.

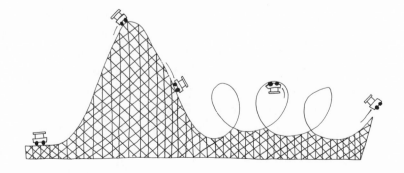

The parking lot is where golfers actually spend most of their time. During their round, they accidentally hit a quote-unquote bad shot, which accidentally hits their partner's brand-new Bentley. Oh, no!

The driving range is the place where golfers test their skills by hitting the ball as hard as they can. The test for accuracy is if they can hit the kid in the armed cart who is driving around picking up the balls. There are little signs that say how far you have hit your ball. Having your ball pass the farthest one is like winning a giant stuffed teddy bear.

The practice green is where you should be spending most of your time before you play. This way, you get a feel for how fast the greens are and how they break. This is a very important place, because if you can't putt, you can't win. The practice green is actually where a lot of action happens. It's where you can watch your partner self-destruct before he even starts playing.

The first thing that you run into when you enter a clubhouse is the locker room. The locker room is a relaxed environment.

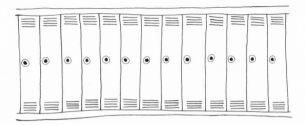

People talk about sports and what happened last night when the Cubs beat the Reds, or how they shot an "85." At school, your locker may hold a math textbook, a journal, and maybe a five-day-old cheese sandwich (not to worry, it's still good under the five-day rule). On a golf course, the lockers are there for golf clothes and golf clubs. You don't need food, because there's always the halfway house.

Next we come to the cart park. Here, the carts frolic in the long grass and have picnics. Just kidding. It actually is where the carts are lined up near the first hole, for you to take off and drive away on your 18-hole road trip. Golf carts look like large, electric go-carts with tops that go at about 15 miles an hour. You can't drive your golf cart on the street because they don't have seat belts, and Safety Sammy says you always have to wear your seat belt while driving on the freeway.

Moving on to the pro shop, we have an opportunity to take a sneak peek at the newest upcoming merchandise for the golf season. If you are in the mood to be a fashion master, you must buy the latest green Versace golf jacket. Or you might be interested in a British Open jug/coffee mug. There are three styles of golf hats to choose from: the baseball cap, the visor, and the Jesper Parnevik, which has a folded-up brim.

They have only created three styles because they don't want to be embarrassed further. You will also find cases and cases of little golf knickknacks. Who buys these things? I don't want to know. Somehow, they have a never-ending supply of golf tees and golf balls. This is what the elves at the North Pole make in the off-season. And if little Andrew was a good boy this year, he will get a brand-new, totally breathable, waterproof, clan MacGregor plaid rainsuit. The fairway is just like the Yellow Brick Road of the *Wizard of Oz*. If you follow it right down the center, you will end up right where you want to be—the center of the green. The hazards on the course play the parts of the Wicked Witch and the flying monkeys. Your job is to be like Dorothy and Toto, and dance your way there, singing the whole way, "There's no place like the 18th hole; there's no place like the 18th hole."

The rough is the area on the golf course that you want to avoid. This is the area that outlines the fairway that is filled with trees, bushes, bunkers, and high grass. It is just like the Amazon jungle, with equally as many dangers. This is where nature comes into play and steals your game. In the rough, seemingly harmless blades of grass can grow titanium hooks that can snag onto your shaft and turn your beautiful 84 into a terrifying 106.

The Rough → named as such for a reason. enter at your own stupidity.

The halfway house is a little restaurant, normally located between the 9th and 10th holes. Since there are 18 holes on a golf course, that is why it is called the halfway house.

It can also be thought of as halfway to beating your partner, halfway to shooting the best round of life, and halfway to going home and taking a nap in front of the TV. The halfway house serves most popular foods of our time. These include cheese sandwiches, fish sandwiches, pickles, saltine crackers, lemonade, potato chips, olives, and those little packets of sugar.

halfway gourmet

cheese sandwich $2.50
fish sandwich $3.50
potato chips $1.00
lemonade $1.00

Unlike the school cafeteria, where they have Argentinian Fridays, during which they serve "chicken" and suspicious yellow rice (which I do not think came from a bottle of Yellow Dye #2, but from Eddie the dishwasher), or mystery meat burgers, at the halfway house you always know what you are dealing with. The halfway house chef is the mastermind behind all these delicious treats. So what if there's an inch of grease on the grill? Just like wine, it ages well.

The next stop on our tour is the caddyshack. Here we find our courageous young heroes, the kings of the greens, the fairway fanatics, and the divot-replacers and clubwashers extraordinaires — their majesties, the caddies. You know why you shot an 85 yesterday? Because of Chris, your caddy. In the caddyshack, the caddies relax, have a soda, and talk about how bad you really played.

And finally, we come to the mothership. **THE CLUBHOUSE**. This is relaxation central for golfers. Imagine a huge treehouse with 24/7 sports channel, stocked with all your favorite things, where nobody can reach you— except without the tree. You get the picture.

One day NASA will send an everyday, normal man who has no flying experience whatsoever to a distant planet. If left to his own devices, the first thing he will set up is a golf club.

# Chapter 11

# The Most Important Things In Golf

T he most important things in golf vary from golfer to
golfer. For some, it's how clean their clubs are, for others
it's winning the Masters. For most golfers, it's something in
between. Nobody ever wants to know what I think the most
important things in golf are, but I'm going to tell you anyway.

One of the most important things in golf is
looking good. It is not a game where your mom
tells you what to wear. You want to pick
your own outfit, because you have to
look stylin' coming down the 18th fairway. That's when everyone looks at you
and says, "Oh wow, he looks really
great," or else, "That was so last
Tuesday." How you look always affects
how you play, at least in my mind. If you
go out on the golf course and you're all dressed up in your
U.S. Open golf hat, your Oakley™ sunglasses, your Dry-Joy™ golf
shoes— of course, your socks have to be low— your Nike™ golf
shirt and your Quicksilver™ shorts, I assure you a good round

of golf. There is a saying, "You look good; you feel good; you play good."

You don't believe me? It's a fact— many great golfers are as well known for how they look as how they play. For instance, Tiger Woods is always seen wearing his very sleek-looking Nike outfits. When he wins, he always wears his classic red shirt and black pants. You may enjoy wearing your pink shirt and yellow pants. I know I do.

David Duval is always winning the British Open wearing his Oakley visors. What would happen if he wore a cowboy hat? Maybe he would be mistaken for Greg Norman.

Greg Norman has great taste on the course. He even has his own line of clothing, named after him, the Shark. He wears those straw cowboy-type hats.

However, even he does not try to wear spurs with his golf shoes.

Jesper Parnevik is Jesper Parnevik. He is the king of style on the golf course. He knows what to wear and when to wear it. He can always be seen wearing those Upper Deck flip-up brim hats. Where does he get them? I must have one. He is also the most colorful of the bunch. It looks like he had a little encounter with the crayon box.

I'm not saying that how they look helped these great golfers play any better. I just like to think of it that way, because it gives me hope.

The second most important thing on a golf course is peace of mind. The golf course is like a giant Dustbuster,

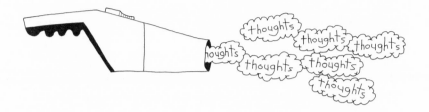

sucking all the thoughts out of your head except golf. Maybe Gandhi should have worked on a golf course. When you're on a golf course, there is no chance of a rock concert being right next door, or a traffic jam going through the 9th and 10th holes, or getting caught in a food fight. When you have peace of mind, you can let your thoughts fly off to places they have never gone before. You may be on the golf course, but your mind might be in Mongolia.

Finally, there is the scorecard. The scorecard keeps track of your total strokes for each hole. This is sort of like your report card for your round. Each hole is like a class, and the scores that you get on each hole are your grades. It is much easier receiving your scorecard than your report card, because it doesn't really matter in later life if you shoot a round of 104.

Your scorecard hopefully won't affect your chances of getting into college. And the best part is, if you get a D on your report card, your parents go crazy, but on a scorecard, no matter what your score is, you won't end up in your room all weekend.

Still, the scorecard is where your game begins, and where your game ends. How can something so little record so many strokes? Imagine the scoreboard at Soldier Field, except you carry it around in your pocket. Without a scorecard, you do not have a score. You can't tell your friends that you shot an

80 without the scorecard to verify it. Professional golfers must turn in an accurate scorecard at the end of their round in a tournament, or they are disqualified. That's how important the scorecard is. Many golfers collect their scorecards to see if they've gotten any worse or any better over the years. They use them to get a handicap. They could also use them to keep track of the number of Rolling Rocks they had last night, or use them as wallpaper in their boom boom room. It's important not to take the scorecard too seriously, because if you take it too seriously, then you're not having fun.

And there's no point in playing golf if you're not going to have fun. Having fun is all about enjoying yourself and being with friends. Without fun, a jungle gym is just a pile of metal. A basketball court is just a wood floor. And a golf course is just a giant backyard.

Which brings me to the absolutely most important thing, the big Bambino and the Cat in the Hat about the game of golf: Have fun!

When you're out on the golf course all by yourself, and nobody else is around, taking as many tee shots as you need is having fun. Playing a round with your friends is fun, no matter what you shoot, because while you're out there, you can talk about stuff that you normally wouldn't because it's private, funny, or even embarrassing. This is the time to tell your friends who you have a crush on, what you really got on your math test, or that you have a weird rash on your butt. It doesn't matter. What happens on the

no, seriously.
come here and
check this out.

golf course stays on the golf course! Most of all, it's fun to do something that you love. Getting a hole-in-one on the first shot could never hurt, either.

A person who loves golf would much rather spend a Saturday playing golf than lying in bed, watching cartoons and eating a box of Lucky Charms.™ Golf is way better than Lucky Charms.™

And that says a lot.

Caddywhack!

# Golf Glossary

### address
This is not the street number where the green is located. This is when you ground your club behind the ball and set your stance and, if you take a swing, no matter what, it counts as a stroke.

### approach shot
This is the shot that you hit when you are expecting to hit it onto the green. Unless you are John Daly, your tee shot is never your approach shot. If you miss the green, too bad. You don't have another approach shot.

### apron
This is what I love to wear when I cook my world-class cheese sandwich. Actually, it's the area in between two bunkers right up against the green, which makes you able to run the ball up the apron and onto the green.

### arc

The arc is how high or how low your shot is. Unless you have a protractor in your golf bag, you can't measure your arc.

### back nine

The last nine holes of your round of golf, or holes 10 through 18. The last nine is crunch time, like the last four hours of school. Here is where you let everything loose. You have to bear down, hit good shots, and hope that they go in the hole. This is where your golf bag becomes 10 pounds heavier.

### back tees

This is extreme golf. This is where the pros play their tee shots from. The back tees are farther away from the hole and positioned so that you must hit a more concise tee shot. Unless you are Tiger Woods, avoid the back tees.

### birdie

A birdie is making one stroke under par for a hole, not your friend Tweetie.

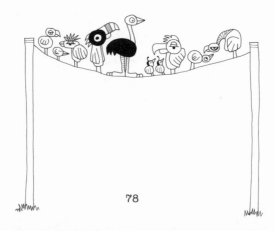

**bogey**

A bogey is making one stroke over par on a hole. This is very scary. This is where the term "bogey-man" comes from, which keeps little kids up at night.

**bunker**

A bunker is another name for a sand trap. It can also be a place to hide when your little brother hits his shot in your direction.

**caddy**

Also known as the golf guru. This person knows every blade of grass on the golf course, and he or she uses this knowledge to help you shoot a great round of golf. Caddies are the true heroes of golf.

**chip**

A chip shot is a low-running, small shot hit just off the edge of the green. They call it a chip because it is to the golf shot as chocolate is to the cookie.

**choke**

This is how low you grip on the club. Where you put your hands on the club can affect how far the ball goes. Of course, on some bad days you might decide to strangle your club. Do not feel guilty; you are not alone.

### cup
The cup is the target, the key place to be on the golf course. The only things that drink out of these are frogs.

### eagle
Making two shots under par on a golf hole. I believe that this shot should be on the back of every quarter.

### flag
The flag is what marks the position of the hole on the green. When you get there, pledge allegiance, for it is your beacon of light in the night which has guided you to safety.

### fore

What you scream out when you hit a bad shot in the direction of other people playing on the course.

### foursome

A group of four golfers playing together in a round of golf. A foursome starts out as friends, but when they end, they are often archenemies.

### fringe

The fringe is the area just off the green that has very short grass. Its job is to stop your ball from getting to the green.

### green

The green has the shortest grass on the golf course. It is just like a carpet in your bedroom. They trim it with cuticle scissors. Just like your last week's science test, the green hides a lot of sneaky breaks, which in this case cause your ball to veer off in funky directions and cause you to miss many putts.

### handicap

The better players on the golf course must play handicapped by carrying an elephant strapped to their back. The worse players get to be carried around in La-Z-Boy chairs by Arnold Schwarzenegger.

### hook

A hook is a shot that you hit with a too inside-out swing which causes the ball to fly in a hook-shaped pattern toward your inside foot. This is most likely to happen when, during your backswing, somehow your foot falls into a ditch made by a salamander. Or at least that's what you can say.

### in play

In play means that your ball is in bounds on the golf course and you can continue to play. Unless the golf course shifts while the ball is in the air.

### lie

This is the type of surface that your ball is sitting on when you play your next shot. You already know all about lies. A good lie is telling your mom that the fruitcake was great. A bad lie is telling your parents that that D was an A. They will hunt you down and find out the truth.

### lip

The edges around the cup. Somehow, the people ahead of me always put glue around the lip of the cup. Does this happen to you?

**mixed foursome**

This is four individuals playing together in a round of golf. They can be anybody. Hope for the best.

**nap**

This is the post-golf ritual. ZZZZ.

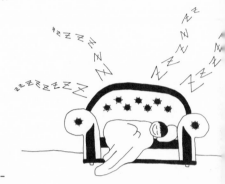

**out of bounds**

When the ball is not in play, but in an area where it cannot be hit, normally resulting in penalty strokes. Watch out for the following: the lake, the clubhouse, the bathroom, birds' nests, or your mom's closet.

**par**

The average number of shots that officials have decided it should take you to get to the hole. There's nothing wrong with being average.

**penalty stroke**

This is the golf equivalent of a time-out in the corner. A penalty is the amount of strokes that you must add to your score after doing something illegal on the course, or hitting a shot out of bounds. This includes picking your ball up off the tee box and placing it in the hole, kicking the ball toward the hole as if it were on a soccer field, or drinking while driving the golf cart.

## PGA

The Professional Golf Association. They are like the Greek Gods at the top of Mount Olympus. Just like the Greek Gods, they can turn themselves into rocks or trees on the golf course. If at any time you are cheating, they will see you. Your punishment will be the Lee Trevino treatment, also known as Mr. Lightning Bolt. And he wasn't even cheating.

### shank

This is when you hit the golf ball off the shaft of the club, causing it to ricochet off an old man's head, not usually into the hole, but into a whole mess of trouble.

### starter

The person who tells you when it is your turn to tee off. Unlike track, he does not hold a gun in his hand and fire it off into the sky. Golf is not a race.

**sudden death**
A play-off between golfers who are tied in
first place in a golf tournament. When you
win a sudden death tournament, you do not
suddenly die— unless your opponents have "accidentally"
smacked you over the head with their putters.

**tee**
A small sliver of wood or plastic on which you balance a golf
ball to prepare it for your tee shot. If your ball won't stay on it,
try using a log.

**topspin**
This never happens, so forget it.

**velocity**
The amount of power behind the golf ball that you have just
hit. Velocity is fun!

**wedge**
A highly-lofted club normally used for short shots around the
green. Please do not attempt to eat.

**yards**
A measurement used by the golf course for how long a hole is.
Hitting a 5-yard drive is bad. Hitting a drive 300 yards is good.

# About The Author

© 2002, Liz Nickles

**D**rew Murray is a 13-year-old who has loved golf since he could pick up a club. He is from the New York area, attends the 8th grade, and lives with his parents and his dog Biscuit. His hobbies include basketball, baseball, singing and as much golf as he can play. He is a member of the Jr. PGA and he aspires to be a professional golfer, sportscaster/writer or a sports agent when he grows up. He is establishing a charitable cause in which kids donate their unused sports collector cards to hospitals, where other children can enjoy them, called "Cards for Kids." He started this book as a card for his favorite golfing partner, his dad. It got too big, and it became *Caddywhack!*

(For more information on "Cards for Kids," or to donate cards, please see the website at www.cardsforkids.org)